The Cats of
Kittyville

Best Friends
ANIMAL SOCIETY

The Cats of
Kittyville

New Lives for Rescued Felines

by Bob Somerville

Introduction by Michael Mountain

President, Best Friends Animal Society

SELLERS
PUBLISHING

Published by Sellers Publishing, Inc.

P.O. Box 818, Portland, Maine 04104
For ordering information: 800-625-3386 toll free
Visit our Web site: www.rsvp.com
E-mail: rsp@rsvp.com

President and Publisher: Ronnie Sellers
Publishing Director: Robin Haywood
Editor-in-Chief: Mark Chimsky-Lustig

ISBN 13: 978-1-4162-0527-2

Library of Congress Control Number
2008928294

10 9 8 7 6 5 4 3 2 1

DESIGN BY MICHAEL HENTGES / BARKING DOG ENTERPRISES. LTD

Printed and bound in Canada

contents

About Best Friends Animal Society 6

Introduction The Wondrous World of Cats

by Michael Mountain, *President*, Best Friends Animal Society 8

Mission Possible Building a Community of Cats 12

Reaching Out to Rescue Second Chances for Cats in Need 34

The Caring Never Stops Lives of Dignity and Love 60

Best Friends Animal Sanctuary, at the heart of southern Utah's national parks, is home to some two thousand abused and abandoned animals: cats, dogs, birds, horses, rabbits and more. Best Friends Animal Society takes animals from other shelters and rescue groups and employs its own rapid response teams to conduct rescues after natural disasters and other major events that put animals in jeopardy.

Cats with special needs of all kinds benefit from Best Friends' expert medical evaluation procedures and ongoing care in Kittyville, the feline section of the sanctuary. Best Friends helped save eight hundred cats from deplorable conditions in a hoarding situation in the Nevada desert in the summer of 2007, an effort widely acclaimed as the Great Kitty Rescue. Hundreds of the cats ended up coming through the sanctuary, and many were adopted or returned to their rightful owners. More than a thousand cats were rescued from the flooded streets of New Orleans after Hurricane Katrina. Members of the Best Friends Animal Help team also work with communities nationwide to arrange spay/neuter and feeding campaigns for feral cats, and they recently helped overturn one small town's institution of a $5 bounty on stray cats, replacing it with a humane solution. Many of the rescued animals who come to Kittyville and other parts of the sanctuary need just a few weeks before they're ready to go to good new homes; others who are sicker or older or have suffered extreme trauma find a home at the sanctuary for the rest of their lives.

Through its volunteer network, Best Friends reaches across the country and beyond to help bring about a time when there will be no more homeless pets. In addition to spay/neuter and feeding programs, Best Friends works with other humane groups to help communities establish foster and adoption programs so that every cat—and every other pet—ever born can be guaranteed a loving home.

LUCY

● DESTRY

Introduction

The Wondrous World of Cats

Michael Mountain

President, Best Friends Animal Society

I'm not sure where Miss Popsicle takes her snooze. It's somewhere in the back room, where I keep piles of old books and boxes and other stuff—but Miss Popsicle considers it her private sanctuary. She's entitled to her secrets, and it would be wrong to go snooping.

In any case, the longer the snooze goes on, the better. Once she wakes up, she'll be screaming for the cat food bowl to be refilled (even though it's still half full) or, if it's late evening and I'm sitting comfortably reading or watching TV, she'll take up a position on the glass table behind and make a flying leap into my lap, where she'll proceed to roll onto her back and wave her paws at me until she begins to slide off and then tries to hang on by deploying all her claws. Amid the commotion that follows, Pudgie, my old Sheltie mix, will wake up, grumble, and make threatening noises at Miss P., who will dance around and then take up a new position on the table. And, in a few minutes, off we go again.

Miss Popsicle is a longish-haired orange female kitty. I once had another long-haired—even longer-haired than Miss P.—orange female called Arabella GingerPop, whom I rescued as a sick stray. Dr. Christy, the Best Friends vet at the time, advised me that she probably wouldn't get too much better or live too much longer. He also mentioned that long-haired orange female cats are quite unusual—a genetic rarity. I took A-Pop, as I would generally call her, home, where the first thing she did was jump on the washing machine. Five minutes later, the washing machine sprang a leak and flooded the room.

Next day, I took her over to the Best Friends clinic, and as we walked in, the main fuse blew and the power went out. Back at home, her long fluffy tail began to lay waste to anything on any table, shelf, or kitchen counter that wasn't nailed down. I began to imagine that she had psychic powers and should be treated as a national treasure . . . or maybe a secret weapon of mass destruction.

Eventually, though, her physical circumstances got the better of her, and one evening she went, as we say here at Best Friends, "over the Rainbow Bridge."

I couldn't imagine that someone with as huge a personality as A-Pop could possibly be limited by something as banal as sickness and death—or even space and time. Surely she still had to be around in some form. Then I read somewhere that the ancient Egyptians believed that the world and the heavens were ringed by a great orange serpent dragon who was the source of all chaos and destruction in the entire cosmos, and whose name was . . . A-Pop.

Everything was now explained. The great, primeval, cosmic force of chaos and destruction had returned as a rare, stray, orange, super-furry, 20th-century cat called Arabella GingerPop. And now I wondered: could there be other such kitties who were equally possessed by the ancient A-Pop?

Tomato the Cat—the investigative reporter for *Best Friends* magazine, whom you'll read about in this book—decided to check the matter out for himself in his regular magazine column. He invited members of Best Friends to let him know if they had ever rescued a long-haired, orange, female kitty or adopted one from their local shelter. And if so, did she, too, have similar powers?

Hundreds of people promptly wrote back with photos of cats they claimed were incarnations of A-Pop. Some fitted the profile to perfection. Others, frankly, weren't long-haired, or weren't female, or weren't even orange. One woman even insisted that her husband, who had ginger hair and was a complete klutz around the house, must be A-Pop.

This all happened many years ago, and I wasn't really thinking about it when I took in Miss Popsicle. She was one of the 295 dogs and cats Best Friends brought over from Beirut during the 2006 war. Animals are always the uncounted "collateral damage" of any war, and the entire country of Lebanon had just one humane society, composed of twelve people—all volunteers. Their three shelters had been destroyed and the animals had nowhere to go. While helping the group reestablish themselves and start some spay/neuter and adoption programs, we brought these cats and dogs back to Best Friends Animal Sanctuary to place them in safe new homes.

So here she is . . . a former street cat from Beirut, rescued by a handful of kind and caring people caught up in a war, who ends up across the ocean in what could only be described as kitty heaven.

Today, as her bushy tail sweeps everything off the table and she takes a flying leap into my lap, using all twenty claws to right herself and settle down for another snooze, I'm thinking, of course, that it was no coincidence when I called her Miss Popsicle. It was, rather, instant recognition. Even though her fur is only medium-long, I think it still qualifies. And this can only mean that, one way or another, A-Pop has made it back . . . yet again.

To some people, homeless cats and dogs are of little value. But to those who are not quite so blind, they are not only precious lives, but also very special beings, blessed with the ability to touch our imagination and lead us into a world of true magic and wonder.

Welcome to Kittyville!

PIGGY

Mission Possible
building a community of cats

There's something that is both soothing and spellbinding about the quality of the light in Angel Canyon. Perhaps it has to do with the stunning red rock cliffs all around ... or the dusky yellow soil ... or the iridescent blue of the sky ... or the shimmering greens of willow and juniper along the creek bed. Whatever it is, the entire landscape seems bathed in an aura of magic and serenity.

The beauty is so mesmerizing that it's easy to feel only the quietness at first. But farther along the road, and up on the mesa above the canyon, another world awaits. It is different and yet somehow the same in its essence. Over the past twenty years, scores of buildings, enclosures, and pastures have filled the terrain with life and activity. Covering more than 3,700 acres, this is Best Friends Animal Sanctuary, the largest no-kill sanctuary in the nation.

Morris (opposite) enjoys a favorite spot on the screened porch of one of Kittyville's main residences. Volunteer Charlotte (below) spends some petting time with three occupants of the Kitty Motel, which houses cats with special needs. Thousands of regular and first-time volunteers share their love in Kittyville every year.

● OLIVER

Escape artist. The picture of innocence, Oliver keeps his true intentions close to the vest. A longtime resident of the WildCats Village, Oliver never missed a chance to sneak past "security" and make a break for the great outdoors. Conquering the challenge seemed to be all he was after: a few yards from the front entrance, he would always hunker down in the sand, waiting patiently to be brought back inside.

Dogs, cats, birds, rabbits, sheep, pigs, and horses inhabit their own special places, and each area has its own unique characteristics.

The section reserved for felines is known as Kittyville, and it can appear as peaceful as any of the surrounding canyonlands at first glance. Its dozen or so buildings look like typical comfortable homes in the Southwestern style, except for large, unadorned screen porches along two or even three walls. Inside the porches are a wild assortment of furnishings: pedestal "trees" with six or seven platforms at different heights; padded houses, some on stilts or stacked one atop another; laundry hampers and plastic tubs with holes cut in their sides stuffed with blankets and other padding; cat beds and scratching posts, small tables topped with washable bath mats, plastic chairs with cat beds on them, and wooden shelving here and there, adorned with pieces of quilting; angled beams and long branches of driftwood serving as ramps to the open rafters; cat toys of every sort—balls of every size and bells and squeaky toys and plastic mice and colorful scraps of felt—scattered absolutely everywhere; and, of course, plenty of litter boxes, some up on shelves or even in the rafters. This is Cat Heaven.

Cats Galore

And there they are, a dozen or more highly contented-looking cats, some peering at you from their own special perches up among the ceiling joists, others rolling around in playful tussles or batting their favorite toy about, still others watching intently from inside cubbyholes, curled up in tight, legs-tucked-in balls of fur. Some have such good hiding places you don't see them right away, until you really look the place over thoroughly. But others come right up to the screen purring, and only the hardest heart could resist walking round to the front door for some closer interaction.

Signs warn visitors to close the door quickly, and the caregivers inside will shout a friendly reminder if they don't hear the click of the latch fast enough. Over at the WildCats Village, despite everyone's best intentions, Oliver sometimes manages to slip between legs and bolt outside. It could hardly be called an escape, though; after a short dash, Oliver collapses into the sand for a back roll—and waits for one of the caregivers to come and "capture" him.

At the Kitty Motel, a special needs building, one of the first cats to greet visitors in the hall is Scooter, a little black fellow with no back legs, who pulls himself swiftly and smoothly across the vinyl flooring and rubs his head against the nearest human leg. Cedric, from the geriatric division, beckons with his regal presence alone, rolling over for a tummy scratch if he feels like it. Weebles, one of the cats known as "neuros"—those with neurological impairments—staggers like a wayward drunk down the hall, sticking close to the wall to keep from falling over; it takes some people aback, until they see that in every other way she acts

Friends indeed. Weebles (below, left) and Maramau share a relaxing moment together in the lobby of the Kitty Motel. By all appearances inseparable, they part ways as soon as a visitor walks through the front door. Maramau has no interest in impressing anyone, but Weebles— whose neurological infirmity causes her to stagger when she walks—likes nothing better than to make her lopsided way across the room in welcome.

● WEEBLES
  & MARAMAU

just like any other affectionate feline. As caregivers here sometimes joke, none of these cats is normal—but only because they don't know anything's wrong with them!

Rooms off the central hall provide housing for other special needs cats in the Kitty Motel: those with feline leukemia or feline immunodeficiency virus (FIV) or the occupants of the Incontinental Suite.

Building Kittyville

These and all the other cats of today's Kittyville are worthy heirs to the cast of feline characters who were part of Best Friends' early days. When they began putting the sanctuary together in the 1980s, the society's founding members—a group of friends from England, America, and elsewhere who had devoted themselves to saving abused, abandoned, and condemned pets—focused their first efforts on building houses for the growing number of dogs they were sheltering. Most of the cats were living in the bunkhouse, which also served as sanctuary office, clinic, and general meeting room, or in people's homes. The first building for cats, the original Kitty Motel, was a rough collection of plywood houses with outdoor areas made of chicken wire stretched between lodgepole pines.

But the rudimentary setting was already being complemented by a host of vivid cat personages. There was, for example, Bruiser, a big tough-looking tom who had taken on the unexpected role of nurturing abandoned litters of kittens. He wasn't physically equipped to feed them, of course, but he did everything else, from grooming to letting them snuggle up against him for naps. One night a starving little cat named Harriet was brought in, her unborn kittens having died because she was too sickly. Bruiser was put in charge of nursing her back to health. She didn't like his

The Kitty Motel. O'Malley surveys the wider world from one of the screened porches of the Kitty Motel, home to cats with special needs. Slanting beams provide access to perches in the rafters; shelves, ledges, and plastic-tub "dens" give the cats additional places to establish their own personal territory.

ministrations at first, digging her claws into his thick fur. He didn't flinch, waiting patiently for her to calm down before resuming his grooming. He cared for Harriet in the bunkhouse for three weeks — at the end of which she was well enough to start returning the favor, licking behind her big friend's ears while he purred and stretched. In the months and years ahead, Bruiser and Harriet were an inseparable team, jointly caring for many orphaned kittens.

Another standout from the early years was Tomato, an orange tabby with respiratory problems. (Apparently he called them his "sneezles.") Michael Mountain took a special shine to Tomato — he seemed to be a classic example of the curious cat, minding everyone else's business for them, appearing and reappearing when least expected. Clearly he needed a job, so Michael appointed Tomato the Cat as *Best Friends* magazine's chief investigative journalist. He proceeded to write pointed articles complaining about the Powers

● THE COLONEL

Top cat. One of Kittyville's most famous citizens, The Colonel first came to the sanctuary from a courtroom. He'd been condemned to death for raiding a neighbor's chicken coop, but Best Friends intervened and got his sentence reduced to "life without parole" in Kittyville. The Colonel — named after Colonel Sanders of fast-food chicken fame — took over the role of Head Cat that once belonged to Benton, ruling the roost with his girlfriend, Jove (opposite).

That Be and hinting that there was a conspiracy going on at Kittyville—one that he was determined to uncover and that possibly included cats everywhere.

There was also Sinjin, the "furry one-eyed pirate," who took charge in the bunkhouse. This feisty little tom had been found on a gravel driveway, horribly burned by some chemical, his pads eaten away right down to the bone; he also had a perforated eye that was being eaten away by parasites. With round-the-clock care, Sinjin had fought his way back to health and now greeted anyone coming into the bunkhouse by jumping up on the kitchen counter and butting his head against the cabinet where he knew all the cat food was. The trick usually worked to the tune of three or four cans a day from gullible passersby.

Head Cat was a title Kittyville's inhabitants seemed to take quite seriously. Although Sinjin was an early candidate for the role, the true first leader was Benton, a furry gray-and-white cat with a useless front leg that had been broken when he'd been hit by a car as he was trying to follow his departing family, who had decided to abandon him when they were moving away. When he waved his little club foot around in front of him, Benton seemed to be commanding his minions, and for the most part, everyone obeyed. His authority and fame assured that when the founders had the resources to construct a new building expressly for special needs cats, there was no doubt that it would be called Benton's House.

As Best Friends grew, more houses were added to Kittyville, including Happy Landings for new arrivals, the WildCats Village for cats from feral colonies who needed special care, a new Kitty Motel for older cats, and several buildings donated by members who had a particular interest in, for example, adoptions, kittens, and cats with feline leukemia. In the adoption house, adorable

THE COLONEL & JOVE

kittens and the most appealing older cats roamed freely among visitors, putting on their charms to win their way into forever homes.

But the Best Friends folk were beginning to notice something they hadn't expected: not only were the cute and cuddly "adoptables" finding new homes, but those who could easily be deemed almost hopelessly unadoptable—the maimed, the chronically ill, the neurologically impaired—were also touching the hearts of Best Friends' growing cadre of members and supporters and being adopted. These special needs cats now all belong to what Best Friends calls the TLC (for "tender loving care") Cat Club, still headquartered at Benton's House. They have a permanent home in the Club if they need it, but most of them soon find their way into loving homes.

Shy Cats

One thing everybody says about Kittyville: it's a very sociable place. The vibe is everywhere. Purring nuzzles abound, and even those who hold themselves a little more aloof, hiding in the rafters and cubbyholes that are part of the design of the rooms, seem members of the overall community. Many of the cats who are brought to Kittyville, especially those who have been victims of trauma, are fearful of trusting others. Indeed, extreme shyness is a common problem, and it poses a real obstacle to adoption, forming a different sort of "special needs" cats. Sometimes cats who have suffered abuse and neglect or who are almost pathologically shy for whatever reason will spit and hiss and keep everyone—other cats and humans too—at bay. No one knew what Will, Kimberly, and Cassie had been through in the past, but they weren't making any progress at the shelter that had been trying to care for them.

To make space for them at the sanctuary Best Friends asked the shelter to take six very sociable and ready-to-be adopted cats in exchange for Will, Kimberly, and Cassie. (These kinds of exchanges are quite common at Best Friends, and help the sanctuary bring in more cats with special needs.) The three newcomers became part of a program dubbed Miss Sherry's Finishing School for Felines, designed by resident animal behavior expert Sherry Woodard to help socialize feral cats and others who have suffered injury or abuse that makes them fearful of humans. The first step is to give them a safe place to be, a limited space usually in the form of a cubby that becomes a private sanctuary. Then, slowly, a caregiver begins the process of socialization. It starts with simply being near the cat, spending time beside the cubby talking gently and soothingly. Then the caregiver will offer a piece of food on the end of a wand so that the cat will learn to associate something good with humans. Next comes soft touching inside the cubby, never going beyond the cat's comfort zone. The caregiver moves on to holding the cat briefly, then for longer periods, and eventually advancing to more playful interactions with toys, other cats, and other people the cat is not familiar with.

As expected, the trio made slow progress at first. Terri Gonzales, a former volunteer now in charge of the Finishing School, explains the approach caregivers take: "If we see that a kitty is not ready to progress, we back up a step and allow them more time. They need to be comfortable and confident every step of the way—this isn't a race."

Progress did come, and Kimberly was the first to take the extraordinary step of going out on an adoption event, followed by Cassie and Will. Meanwhile, Lily and Baker, two of the cats

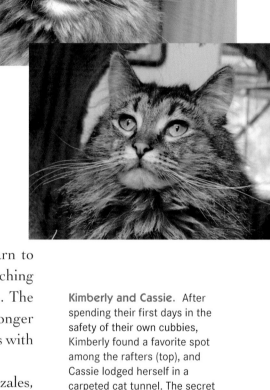

Kimberly and Cassie. After spending their first days in the safety of their own cubbies, Kimberly found a favorite spot among the rafters (top), and Cassie lodged herself in a carpeted cat tunnel. The secret to breaking through their shyness was respecting their personal territory; caregivers then slowly and carefully made bonds with gentle words of encouragement and soft petting when the cats felt comfortable.

● FINISHING SCHOOL CATS: SNOOPY, GUS & CARSON

from Kittyville who'd traded places with Will, Kimberly, and Cassie, were adopted almost right away. Of the Finishing School's success, Sherry notes, "So far, with our encouragement, and by starting out with limiting the cats' space, not a single cat has declined our offer to start learning how to be a housecat—again or for the first time."

Spotlight on: **Oscar**

Oscar's problem wasn't shyness—far from it. Indeed, he was more on the bully end of the spectrum. It wasn't other cats he bullied, though. Oscar seemed to have a knack for terrifying people. His story exemplifies the Best Friends solution to the plight of many cats with aggressive behavior problems. Because of their behavior they tend not to be adopted, and then they run out of time at shelters that aren't firmly committed to a no-kill approach. At Best Friends, though, there's no clock running. Again, it isn't a race.

Oscar was a large, sleek, black cat who lived in Saudi Arabia, in the gated compound for a major oil company's employees. He was strictly an outdoor cat, living a semi-feral life in the backyard of one particular house. When a couple named Ron and Bonnie moved in, Bonnie began feeding him and trying to encourage him to come into the house every so often. She would bang on his metal food dish and call, "Oscar! Oscar! Dinnertime!!" and when he approached, she would use the food to entice him inside. Over time he became more comfortable indoors, sometimes spending the day curled up on a couch or snuggled in near Bonnie's side. He even started sleeping at the foot of the bed. He still wasn't comfortable with other people, but Bonnie had won his heart.

Kits of a feather. Curious kittens perch on pedestals and shelving in Morgaine's Place, donated by a family in memory of their beloved cat. Morgaine's Place has a wing for kittens needing special care, and another for highly adoptable cats. Of course, Best Friends prides itself on finding homes for older cats too, as well as those with special needs.

Then one evening Ron and Bonnie were hosting a diplomatic reception, and some very eminent types were in attendance. Oscar was safely tucked away in the bedroom but then somehow got out. Chaos ensued, as a frightened—and frightening—Oscar started flying all over the place, Bonnie in full pursuit. She finally caught up with him, but when she grabbed for him, he sank his teeth deeply into her hand, causing a wound so serious that she had to go to the emergency room.

The rules were very strict in Saudi Arabia about such situations, and despite the fact that Ron and Bonnie wanted to keep Oscar, the authorities were insisting that he be put down. Bonnie was distraught, until she remembered about Best Friends. She and Ron had visited the sanctuary once and knew about their work. Bonnie had an idea, and she proposed it to the veterinarian in charge of Oscar's case: could she send Oscar to Best Friends and thus save his life? The vet said he could only agree if Best Friends promised in writing that Oscar would be kept at the sanctuary for the rest of his life and never adopted.

After a few phone calls and a mountain of paperwork, Oscar boarded

● OSCAR & TWO FRIENDS

a flight to Amsterdam, and then Los Angeles, and two days later, he arrived at Kittyville. At first he seemed to have reverted again, snarling whenever someone even tried just talking to him. The caregivers didn't feel they could trust him around other cats either, so he was kept in a solitary enclosure near the bunkhouse. After two weeks he still wasn't making any progress. So the Best Friends staff decided to take a chance that, looking back, can only be called inspired wisdom. There was a frail and timid little cat named Heidi, a rescued stray, who wasn't doing well in a group setting and consequently was eating so little she was almost starving herself to death. Heidi was brought over to Oscar's enclosure, safely ensconced in her own house, and a bowl of food was set down. Oscar went right for it, eating most of it. He stretched out for a while, then came back to the food and picked up a mouthful; was he going to take it all for himself? Instead, he walked over to the door of Heidi's house and gently laid the mouthful of moist food right under her nose. She nibbled away, and when that was finished, he brought her another, and then another until the bowl was clean.

It was the beginning of a beautiful friendship, and a transformation for both cats. Heidi became less timid, and Oscar softened again. He went on to live ten more years at Best Friends, at one stage occupying the lofty position of Chief of Stuff for The Colonel, who had won election as Head

On the road. Oscar goes for a walk with a suitably attired companion (opposite). He first came to the sanctuary as a reprieve after falling afoul of the authorities during a diplomatic reception in Saudi Arabia when he bit a member of his human family in a moment of panic.

● OSCAR

Cat in 2000. (Oscar's title came from his propensity for collecting other cats' toys, pencils and pens, and pretty much anything he laid his paws on.) Oscar spent his last year in foster care with a staff member. When he finally passed "over the Rainbow Bridge," as Best Friends folks like to say, he took an honored spot at Angels Rest, the memorial grove at the sanctuary, where hundreds of wind chimes ring with every passing breeze.

Spotlight on: **Roo**

A problematic temperament isn't the only difficulty cats come to Best Friends with, of course. For reasons that aren't immediately apparent, cats seem to be frequent targets of torture and physical abuse, and perhaps because of their known ability to survive on their own, they are often considered disposable. Sometimes rescuers never know what caused the horrendous injuries they find. They only know they have to do whatever they can to help.

Little Roo, a tiger-striped kitten, was found in a park in Scipio, Utah, about two hundred miles north of the sanctuary, by a woman who had heard him gently meowing in the grass. The tiny kitten was in dreadful shape: both of his front legs were completely gone, leaving only ragged, bloody stumps; part of his tail was missing; and he had several nasty cuts across his body. Perhaps he'd been the victim of a lawn mower, but whatever had happened, his rescuer was desperate. She couldn't afford to pay a vet but she knew about Best Friends, so she gave them a call.

Roo was just the kind of case Best Friends is all about. The sanctuary gets hundreds of applications from individuals every week to have animals placed with them and can only accept a very few, so it typically focuses on special situations—and Roo was certainly one of those.

Despite the pain he was obviously suffering, Roo proved his spunk right from the start, sitting up in his crate on his hind legs almost like a kangaroo on the lookout (it's how he got his name). The Best Friends clinic gave him prompt attention, first to stabilize his vital signs, which were at low ebb from shock and loss of blood. Then he received a transfusion, had his wounds cleaned, and was treated with both topical and intravenous antibiotics. Surgery to remove dead tissue around the stumps and to close his cuts would come later, when he was strong enough to tolerate anesthesia.

Roo went into foster care at night when the clinic was closed with Mike Bzdewka and his wife, Shelli, who had been caregivers at Best Friends for several years. Mike had at one time been the manager of Kittyville but had gone back to caregiving, preferring as much hands-on work with the cats as he could get. He and Shelli fell for Roo right away, admiring his obvious determination. He didn't like to be picked up, perhaps because it was painful, so they quickly learned to comfort him with head and chin scratches. Roo was soon staying with them all the time, going back to the clinic only for the three rounds of surgery he needed to repair all his wounds and for checkups.

His adaptability to the circumstances life had thrust upon him proved remarkable. He couldn't get into the litter box by himself, so Shelli or Mike would lift him in, but he'd have to learn how to use

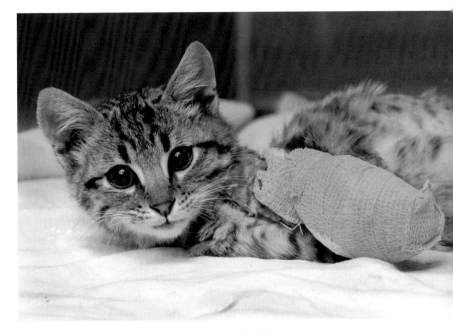

● ROO

In the pink. Roo recovers from surgery to his left front leg. He was brought to Kittyville after being discovered in a park with horrible injuries to both front legs, possibly having been run over by a lawn mower. His indomitable spirit shines through in his big, curious eyes.

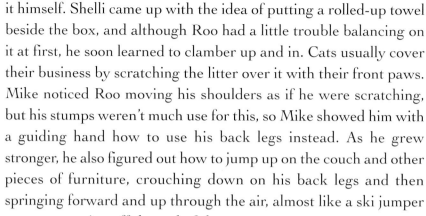

On the mend. His stitches still in place, Roo sits up in a characteristic pose. The attempt to preserve some of his left leg for a possible prosthesis failed, and later surgery removed the remaining stump. Roo came through it all, ever eager to explore a world filled with loving human companions.

it himself. Shelli came up with the idea of putting a rolled-up towel beside the box, and although Roo had a little trouble balancing on it at first, he soon learned to clamber up and in. Cats usually cover their business by scratching the litter over it with their front paws. Mike noticed Roo moving his shoulders as if he were scratching, but his stumps weren't much use for this, so Mike showed him with a guiding hand how to use his back legs instead. As he grew stronger, he also figured out how to jump up on the couch and other pieces of furniture, crouching down on his back legs and then springing forward and up through the air, almost like a ski jumper going off the end of the ramp.

After weeks of recovery and months of adapting to life as a growing cat, Roo developed a troublesome digestive problem, throwing up fairly frequently after he was done with his meals. Several tests and examinations showed nothing unusual medically, so Mike tried elevating his food bowl, placing it on top of a tall jar. This allowed Roo to eat sitting up, rather than hunched over, precariously balanced on his back legs. For reasons that weren't entirely clear, the change in position seemed to help, and Roo eventually got over his digestive difficulties.

Roo was quite popular throughout the Best Friends family of caregivers and volunteers. He also became the inaugural feline member of the Guardian Angel program, which allows members to support the special care of animals like Roo and follow their progress on regularly updated blogs. Roo certainly wasn't being overlooked. Shelli kept everyone up to date on his progress through the online journal, and soon adoption applications were pouring in—in record numbers as it turned out.

ROO

The only problem would be finding just the right forever family for Roo. Beth and Joanne, who lived in New York, had put in an application, and when Beth came to visit, Mike and Shelli knew almost right away that they were the ones. Beth and Joanne had several other special needs cats at home—one with only three legs, another blind in one eye, another with a hearing problem—so they would almost certainly be ready to handle anything that came up with Roo. Mike and Shelli and the others at Best Friends who were deciding on the adoption applications virtually had that decision made for them when they saw Beth holding Roo for the first time. This little cat, who often didn't like to be held, snuggled into the safety of Beth's arms and began purring.

Things moved quickly from there, and Beth took Roo to his forever home a few days later. She sent in steady reports, and there were no doubts from anyone that Roo was where he belonged. A few months later, Beth wrote in Roo's online journal, "In the morning I just look at him and melt. After I get done ogling over him, he usually stands straight up like a prairie-dog, looks around, bee-bops down the stairs, and jumps back up on his cat tree to start the day all over again. A cat's life . . . huh!"

A cat's life richly deserved, and one made possible by Best Friends and the caring community called Kittyville.

Shelli, Roo's foster mom, plants a loving kiss.

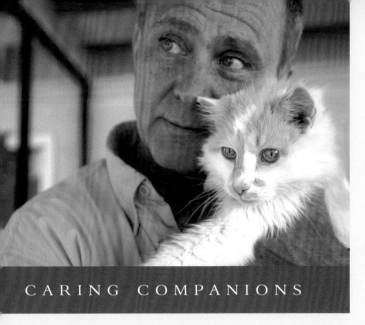

CARING COMPANIONS

ironman of kittyville

Bob Johnson was working as a stockbroker when something about a Best Friends flyer struck him and he decided to pursue a nagging thought. As he puts it, "I was an animal guy working with money people. I had to go out and find a place to leave my legacy." He took a trip out to the sanctuary, just to see what the possibilities were, and had a lightbulb moment during his first visit to some of the buildings of Kittyville. "I was flabbergasted. I thought the animals would be in these cages. I didn't know there'd be these kinds of buildings. This is what I was meant to do."

Bob was hired as a caregiver and has a truly astounding record that makes him the Cal Ripken of Kittyville's human crew: in seven years taking care of cats, he has missed only three days of work. And equally astounding is all he does. Bob likes to get to his corner of Kittyville, the Colonel's Barracks at the WildCats Village, at three in the morning, when no one else is around and it's just himself and the cats. Part of the reason has to do with his particular charges—former alley cats and ferals, as well as house-cats that are uncomfortable around people. But it's easy to see that Bob relishes these times just as much. In the quiet of the early early morning, the cats come out to greet him: first Baxter and

Sammy, then Bob's special girlfriend, Kaylie, who will follow him around all day; and then the rest—Cheeze, Joni, Clowny, Wallace and his sidekick Dusty, Harrison, Solomon . . . and more and more and more. Bob knows them all by name, and there are about twenty cats in each of the building's six rooms. "They know I'm their daddy. I have the food and the treats and the clean beds for them," he says.

Like other caregivers, Bob has a busy time for hours, doing laundry, sweeping porches, mopping every inch of floor, and wiping every surface down. He changes all the litter boxes, some of which are up on ledges near the rafter perches the shyest cats prefer. He makes specialized meals, dispenses medication, and keeps an eye on everybody. When Baxter came back from a few days at the clinic, Bob kept watch on him and Graham, a some-what bossy new arrival. All was well, as it usually is; as Bob points out, they tend to work things out themselves. Bob's seen only three fur-flying fights in all his years, and they were basically over before he had to intervene.

According to Bob, even the most frightened new cats tend to adjust quickly and fit right in with the group. He keeps his pockets full of treats to help bring shy ones out of their shells and employs a lot of patience as well. Soothing words, gentle proffers of treats, and time all work wonders. And there are many reward-ing transformations. The most sociable cats get hallway privileges and greet visitors with leg rubs and purring.

Bob's love affair with cats began when he was an adult and a couple of strays stole his heart. He now has four cats at home—three that he adopted from Best Friends and another stray who adopted him. His days at Kittyville are long, the work tiring and often emotional, even when the event is the happy one of adoption. "The cats are my family," Bob says, "and I hate to see them go, but they live forever in my heart."

● ANDY

SPEEDY

Reaching Out to Rescue
second chances for cats in need

Cats have been part of the human family since the beginnings of civilization. They were among the first creatures represented in art and were revered in ancient Egypt. They have been the companions of emperors and empresses, the beloved pets of little girls and boys, the wandering vagabonds of our cities and towns, using their smarts to survive the urban "wilds." They are affectionate and aloof, doting and independent, frolicsome and serene—indeed running a whole wide gamut of personalities.

But one common quality seems to be an air of competence. Cats know how to fend for themselves, in virtually any conditions—at least that's the impression they often give. The truth of the matter is that they need far more from us than we realize. In a way, they ask more from us than dogs do. They ask us to be

Sherry Woodard (opposite), Best Friends' animal behavior consultant, feeds cats rescued from a hoarding situation in the Nevada desert. More than a hundred of the cats were brought to Kittyville, including Andrew (below, with caregiver Brianne), who recovered quickly and was adopted in the spring of 2008.

their helpmates and to allow them their independence at the same time. They ask us to coddle them and to give them free rein. Where people sometimes go wrong with cats is in not understanding the nuances of that delicate balance. And the consequences of that lack of understanding are the abandonment and abuse of thousands upon thousands of cats across the country, and even on occasion well-meaning but ultimately misplaced interference in their natural lives.

Time and again, Best Friends reaches out to these felines, rescuing and comforting and rehabilitating where appropriate, but also allowing some of them the freedom they need.

The Great Kitty Rescue

In July of 2007, a volunteer for a supposed animal shelter near the town of Pahrump, Nevada, tipped off local officials about abysmal conditions at the facility, located on two acres of desert scrubland a few miles from Death Valley. Animal control officers arrived just before noon on a blistering-hot day to take possession of the site and all the imprisoned cats. Ten minutes later, animal control handed the operations to Best Friends, who had an emergency crew staged on the edge of the property. The officers said there were about four hundred cats on the grounds, many of them sick and all of them in need of immediate care. As it turned out, there were more than seven hundred cats and kittens, with an additional one hundred at the house of the facility's former director. Russ Mead, Best Friends' general counsel, who set up the rescue center after Hurricane Katrina in New Orleans and was now doing the same at Pahrump, commented, "In a way, this is worse than Katrina. This was caused by humans, and the animals are in worse shape."

Cats seemed to be everywhere, most of them outside on the bare desert sand, with temperatures soaring to almost 120 degrees

Hoping for help. An orange tabby (opposite) looks out over a sea of other felines at the site of the Great Kitty Rescue near Pahrump, Nevada, where daytime temperatures sometimes reach 120 degrees. This kitten was in better shape than many of the others, who were suffering from various illnesses and had been underfed and living in filthy conditions.

Coming around. Some Great Kitty Rescue cats were so traumatized that they hid from their human helpers wherever they could (above). But food worked its inevitable magic. Best Friends brought in chow by the caseload (right), and many of the cats soon lost their fear. As Barbara Williamson, one of the Best Friends rescuers, put it, "Maybe it speaks to the inherent regal nature of a cat, that as terrified, starved, and sick as they were, these cats were always true to themselves and nobly invited us in."

during the day and virtually no shade. The smell of urine and feces was overpowering, and there was little evidence that the animals were being routinely fed or given clean water. Many of them were clearly on their last legs, and indeed some either died or had to be euthanized in the next days and weeks. Most of the survivors were either sick with respiratory problems and more serious illnesses such as feline leukemia and FIV, or they were emaciated, starving, and filthy.

The Best Friends rescuers got to work immediately. Fresh food and water was put out, the dozen or so ramshackle sheds on the property were power-washed and sterilized with bleach, and well-fenced runs were built so that the cats could be separated into smaller colonies numbering about twenty-five animals apiece. The goal was to stop the further spread of infection, to keep true ferals together, and to begin a systematic process of medical exams, vaccinations, and behavioral evaluations. More than one hundred of those in the very worst shape were taken back to the Angel Canyon sanctuary in Utah. Others were placed with reputable local shelters, and the rest were kept at the Pahrump facility and looked after by a dedicated team of caregivers, vets, and volunteers. The Great Kitty Rescue was well under way.

Meanwhile, legal precautions were pursued to ensure that the owner of the property wouldn't be able to reclaim any of the animals. What the authorities were dealing with was a classic case of hoarding, a recognized psychological disorder in which people have an uncontrollable compulsion to collect many more animals than they could ever possibly care for. Hoarders profess a love of animals and contend that they are rescuing them and saving their lives, but their actions speak otherwise, as the Pahrump facility made painfully clear. As Russ

Continuing care. Although the cats in the worst shape were brought to Best Friends almost immediately after the Great Kitty Rescue began in the summer of 2007, caregivers and volunteers remained at the compound for more than six months, caring for all the others who were being given more time to readjust to a normal life.

Mead put it, "Hoarders have the potential to harm hundreds of animals at a time while sometimes hiding behind the no-kill movement, declaring nonprofit status, and keeping the public away from the facility. Animal hoarders can be members of the chamber of commerce while the animals in their care are suffering silently."

As it turned out, many of the Pahrump felines were not, as the hoarders had insisted, rescued strays or feral cats at all, but lost housecats who had, in effect, been kidnapped. Some even had microchips and other means of identification and were able to be returned to their families. A woman named Jeanette, from Las Vegas, had lost her two cats, Cabbie and Chaos, two years before, and had been told that someone had been trapping cats nearby, but she had never been able to find out more. She had given up hope. When Best Friends called to tell her they had two microchipped cats at Pahrump who were registered in her name, she started to cry, then said she was on her way. The reunion moved everyone, and Jeanette's heart was big enough to take on another cat as well, Onyx, who had apparently become fast friends with Cabbie and Chaos during their time together.

Reunion. Jeanette clutches her beloved Chaos. She had lost him and her other cat, Cabbie, more than two years earlier when they suddenly disappeared from her Las Vegas neighborhood. It turned out they had been trapped and brought to the Pahrump compound by the animal hoarders who ran the supposed shelter. She got both of them back.

Other cats at Pahrump who appeared to be feral at first reverted to friendly, approachable felines almost right away. "If you hold them like a baby, with their belly up, a lot of them just become limp in your arms," said Sherry Woodard, Best Friends' animal behavior consultant. Many of these cats were put up for adoption and readily found new homes with families who had heard the news and wanted to help.

Still, there were many, many more who had to recover from illnesses and from the effects of the cruel neglect they had suffered. And that's how Miss Sherry's Finishing School for Felines first came into existence.

Spotlight on: **Kermit**

Sherry was heartened by how quickly some of the traumatized cats were turning back into "pussycats," responding positively to human contact. "That part is really fun to watch, that they're starting to enjoy being around people," she said to one of the many news people who came out to do live reports. But she was also encountering dozens who clearly needed more help getting reaccustomed to a human presence in their lives. She arranged for these fearful ones to be brought back to the Best Friends sanctuary, and she and fellow Pahrump rescuer Terri Gonzales got the Finishing School up and running.

One of the cats brought from Pahrump was an extremely shy little orange cat named Kermit, noteworthy for his crinkly ears. He was so withdrawn at first that his caregivers said they couldn't even get a good look at him because he would always curl up and hide himself away wherever he could. He clearly wasn't ready for the Finishing School initially, but after a few days of settling in, he joined twenty-five others—Angelina, Audrey, Bagara, Bambino, Bubbles, Bunny, Carson, Dice, and so on down the list to Sylvester, Tazo, Zappa, and Ziplock—in the hurriedly put-together yurts (tentlike buildings that had been invaluable during the Hurricane Katrina rescue) that became the Finishing School's campus at Kittyville. Each yurt was divided into three main areas, known as the classroom, the playroom, and the real life room. The classroom was essentially a collection of individual cubbies where the cats had the

Kermit was among the Great Kitty Rescue cats brought to Kittyville for rehabilitation. He was so frightened at first that he couldn't be handled and spent all his time cowering in his cubby. Eventually he joined other cats in the socialization program at the sanctuary, known as Miss Sherry's Finishing School for Felines.

KERMIT

security of their own private space and where they started to learn to accept human contact—first just the presence of a person nearby, then gradually some hand feeding, some petting, and eventually being held in a lap. Next they got to try the playroom, where they could interact more freely with caregivers, volunteers, and other cats. The final step up was to the real life room, complete with furniture, laptop computers, other everyday objects, and even a couple of small dogs—including Sherry's own Miles. The idea, of course, was to get them fully adapted to life in a forever home.

Terri and her team gave the cats all the time they needed to advance from room to room. Kermit was still very withdrawn at first, but in a few days he started to make progress, and was eventually moved from one section of the play area he had grown comfortable with to another. That's when his fascinating, endearing personality, hidden previously in the shadow of lingering fear, began to shine.

Kermit seemed to be missing a favorite cat tree scratching post that was in the other area he'd been in. No one realized this at first, but Kermit found a way to get his point across. Bob and Corinne, two volunteers visiting from San Diego, were working at the Finishing School and noticed that every time they passed by Kermit, he would meow at them with a sad, almost begging tone. They tried different toys...different treats...and eventually figured out that what he really wanted was his scratching post, which was still in his old room. The Finishing School was supposed to be about training the cats, but clearly Kermit was the one doing the training. Bob and Corinne were so taken with his antics that, after a test-run sleepover in their RV, they filed the paperwork to adopt him.

Kermit and his funny little ears now reside happily in San Diego with new big brother cat Sal and a new cat tree. As Bob and Corinne note in his online journal, it's his new "Furrever Home."

Bob and Corinne start the bonding process with Kermit, who seemed to have picked them out to be his forever family when they were volunteering at the Finishing School. Best Friends' patient approach had succeeded in transforming the once-withdrawn Kermit into a lovable feline full of personality.

Maynard (left) and Little Mister, rescued by a shelter in St. George, Utah, were brought to Kittyville because the shelter was unable to care for their special needs. Both suffering neurological impairments, the two are known affectionately as the Tortoise and the Hare; Maynard (the Hare) dashes and scrambles all over the place, while Little Mister (the Tortoise) moves deliberately but always manages to catch up to his friend.

Spotlight on: **Loverboy**

Reacquainting themselves with human companionship wasn't the only challenge facing cats from the Great Kitty Rescue. For many of them, regaining health was the more serious hurdle. And perhaps no other cat from Pahrump faced bigger challenges than Loverboy.

Loverboy was in dreadful shape when Shelley, a member of the Great Kitty Rescue team, came upon him. He weighed only six pounds when he should have been twice that, with almost no fur on him. He was also very ill and had an empty look in his eyes that he shared with many of those who'd been rescued, as if he couldn't relate to anything going on around him.

He had to be force-fed at first, but Shelley also arranged for him to have a very soft bed in his cubby, and she would talk to him gently every day—the classic Best Friends combination of ensuring privacy and encouraging contact that works so well with cats in trauma. Loverboy was a tough case, though. Shelley remembers, "He would look up as if to say, 'Are you talking to me? And why?'"

The breakthrough started when Shelley placed a homemade catnip toy in front of him on the third day. After a moment or two, he reached out and very slowly cupped his paw around it, pulling it in close. "The next morning, he was still holding the toy," Shelley recalls. "He had not moved. That day I held him close and although it was tough to pet anything but bones, he

● LOVERBOY

received a lot of loving and cooing. When I put him back in his cubby, he ate."

Fast-forward to a visit Shelley paid to Loverboy at Kittyville. She hadn't seen him for six months (during which his care had continued at Best Friends), and she almost couldn't believe her eyes. "My breath caught in my throat. He was beautiful!" He had gained back four pounds and was far from the sack of bones he'd been, with a full face and better yet a full coat of fur. But even more significant was the transformation in his whole being.

LOVERBOY

"Loverboy pressed his head into my hand," Shelley recalls, "and rubbed one side of his head against my palm and then began head-butting my hand and arm. He stood up and came closer, which was my cue to pick him up." The resilient little survivor had come through the intervening time, weathering ongoing illness, clearly determined to get the most out of life. There was never any quit in him.

"Looking into his eyes, I felt I could still see a hint of the devastation that once was," Shelley says of that day. "But greater than that was a new and brighter look of hope. Loverboy looked over my shoulder at the cat next door. Ah, so it's true, I thought. You do have a girlfriend."

Loverboy's story shows just how powerful the effect of Best Friends' care can be. When he was first brought from Nevada to Kittyville, he got the standard battery of tests and came up positive for feline immunodeficiency virus (FIV), which would make his recovery medically more challenging. The loss of fur had been caused by ringworm, which was treated with an anti-fungal cream and other medication, but because his immune system was compromised by the FIV, the ringworm returned and had to be treated again. The same thing happened with a bacterial ear infection he also suffered—it was cured, then recurred, and then it was cured again. He also had to have major dental work.

Many people wrongly assume that FIV cats have to be isolated and thus stand little chance of being adopted. First of all, FIV cannot be transmitted to humans, and it can only pass from cat to cat through a serious bite. Loverboy thus had two things going in his favor—an exceptionally gentle nature and virtually no teeth!

Loverboy took up residence in the office of Bobbie Foster, manager of Kittyville, and he continued to charm his many admirers through his online journal. One of his fans was a woman named Hannah, a former veterinary assistant who had previously integrated an FIV kitten into what she calls "my general cat population at home." One day she was looking at Loverboy's journal, and his most recent picture struck a chord. "Ten minutes later I was sending an email asking to adopt him .... How could you not love a cat with those eyes? And there was this dignity that radiated from the screen."

Bobbie Foster went the extra mile—to be precise, almost eight hundred miles—for Loverboy, driving him to his new forever home near San Francisco. It was yet another happy ending for the cats of Pahrump. A year after they were rescued from hoarding hell, only a few dozen remained at Kittyville, happily living their reclaimed lives.

Office boy. Loverboy's beguiling eyes—one green, one blue—work their magic on Bobbie Foster, manager of Kittyville, as he hangs out in her office with another Great Kitty Rescue cat, Miss Atlanta.

Keeping Faith with Ferals

The situation at Pahrump highlights a common misconception about cats who are fearful around humans. Traumatized cats often have this kind of reaction, but it by no means indicates that they are what animal behaviorists refer to as true ferals. The difference goes far beyond mere semantics. Abused or traumatized domesticated cats, strays who have been away from humans for a while, and housecats who have been abandoned by their families need the kind of resocialization that Miss Sherry's Finishing School is all about. Ferals, on the other hand, require different approaches that acknowledge their inherent nature. Best Friends does its utmost to embrace all these needs. The complex of buildings at Kittyville known as the WildCats Village, for example, was specifically designed for feral cats who—because their colonies have been wiped out or because they have illnesses or injuries and can no longer survive on their own—need the special, tailored care Best Friends can provide.

But what, precisely, are feral cats? Most feral colonies begin with cats who were abandoned by their human families or strayed away and then learned to adapt to life on the streets. Their kittens and future generations grow up without being socialized with humans and behave more like urban wildlife—wary of people but still dependent on them for food and care. The resulting communities can maintain themselves for generations and in some places have almost achieved the status of cultural icons. Rome is famous for its feral colonies, thought to number in the thousands.

Not all feral colonies are stable, though, and in some environments their populations can grow to a point that threatens the health of the individual cats. Best Friends and other humane groups support a population control method known as trap-neuter-return, or TNR. Caregivers—often local cat lovers who have been

A **feral cat** (opposite) watches the goings-on in his territory. Feral cats are usually strays or abandoned pets who have adapted to living on their own, often in colonies. They tend to avoid contact with humans.

feeding feral colonies and providing outdoor shelters—trap the cats, take them to veterinarians to be spayed or neutered and for shots and a health check, and then return them to their colony (vets take off the tip of one ear so that already-altered animals can be easily identified). TNR programs allow ferals to live out their lives without changing their basic nature, and they gradually reduce the numbers.

The one "solution" that doesn't work for ferals is capturing them and placing them in local shelters. Although it might on the surface sound more humane than poisoning or otherwise eliminating colonies outright, ferals in shelters almost never get adopted and inevitably end up being killed. Early in 2008, the town council of Randolph, Iowa, chose to handle its feral cat problem by instituting a $5 bounty on every stray brought to the town shelter, thinking it was the kindest way to address citizens' concerns about feral cats in their neighborhoods.

When Best Friends and other like-minded groups heard about the bounty, they got in touch with the mayor and other officials and explained the virtues of a well-managed TNR program. To their credit, town leaders listened and shortly thereafter repealed the bounty. Best Friends and other groups then sent caregivers to Randolph to get the TNR up and running, with the ultimate goal of turning over its management to local caregivers and cat lovers who would monitor the existing colonies to ensure that the cats remained healthy and safe. The outcome was that a well-meaning but misguided approach was transformed into one that worked even more effectively and that respected both the needs of the human community and the inherent dignity of the ferals. Indeed, within a few weeks, other towns in the region were in touch with Best Friends about setting up TNR programs in their own communities.

Helping ferals. The best approach for feral cats depends on their circumstances. The cat opposite is part of a stable colony being maintained through a trap-neuter-return program managed by Best Friends. The affectionate pair below were among the eight hundred cats of the Great Kitty Rescue. With no existing colony to which they could be returned, these and other ferals from Pahrump were either socialized through the Finishing School or given permanent sanctuary at Kittyville's WildCats Village.

● JAZZ

Spotlight on: **Jazz**

Dealing with hoarding situations, returning kidnapped housecats to their people, rehabilitating traumatized cats, setting up TNR programs, providing sanctuary at the WildCats Village for ferals with special needs—rescue comes in many forms whenever the caregivers of Kittyville are involved. Sometimes their efforts go unheralded, which is just fine as far as the people at Best Friends are concerned; saving lives, finding forever homes, and preserving the dignity of animals are genuinely all that really matters to them. Sometimes, though, the good work plays out on a more prominent stage. In 2006, for example, Best Friends helped rescue 145 cats from the war-torn streets of Beirut, Lebanon, and later that year took part in saving animals from the devastation wrought by a massive earthquake in Peru; both these efforts garnered international attention. But by far the most well-known and widely acclaimed of Best Friends' many rescue operations happened in the Gulf Coast region around New Orleans after Hurricane Katrina in 2005.

Best Friends helped rescue more than six thousand animals from the flooded streets of New Orleans. Most of them were dogs—simply because dogs would bark and even swim out to the boats. Cats, on the other hand, were hard to find and even harder to rescue, often dashing back to hiding places when they saw people approaching. The Best Friends teams eventually employed humane traps baited with food to recover more than a thousand cats from in and around the city.

By December, three months after the hurricane, fewer and fewer cats were being found, and those who were recovered turned out to be in pretty bad shape. It seemed at times that the work was done, but then one day rescuers came upon a sad cat who was later named Jazz. He was found in a trailer park, his eyes crusted over so that he couldn't see a thing. He also had a couple of nasty

Jazz (opposite) hangs out on a favorite shelf in one of the porches of the Casa de CalMar. The skin below his eyes still shows signs of the surgery that was performed to keep his eyelids from rolling inward. Casa de CalMar was built by a member of Best Friends (Cal) in memory of his wife (Martha) as a special care home for cats with feline leukemia and FIV.

wounds behind his ears. He was starving and hurting and required immediate attention.

By this time in the rescue effort, a staging area called Celebration Station had been set up in Metairie, on the north side of the city. Jazz's visible wounds were treated and his overall health was evaluated there. A vet determined that the problem with his eyes was that his eyelids were rolled inward, a condition known as entropion that causes painful lesions; in Jazz's case the lesions had ulcerated and crusted over. He also had a nasty respiratory infection and to top things off tested positive for both feline leukemia and FIV. The decision was made to send him to the clinic at Best Friends for more intensive care.

Jazz was understandably withdrawn when he first arrived at the clinic, but the most important thing was treating his physical ailments. Antibiotics helped both the respiratory infection and the wounds behind his ears, and soothing drops provided relief for his eyes. But the staff at the clinic wanted to help his spirit recover as well, so they continually talked comfortingly to him in his cubby, and over the course of a week or two, this gorgeous fellow began to come out of his shell. He started "talking" to his caregivers, meowing and purring, and when they opened his crate, he would come forward and nuzzle his head into the nearest hand. There was no question from his response that he loved getting his head rubbed and would purr away for minutes on end.

A month later, Jazz was well enough to undergo surgery to correct his eye problem. He would no longer suffer the painful irritation of eyelashes rubbing against his eyes. The Jazz Man, as everyone had taken to calling him, was clearly on the road to a happier life. After recovering from the surgery, he moved into one of the houses for feline leukemia cats. He took to hanging out by himself in the rafters at first, but soon made fast friends with a

JAZZ

Mischief eyes. The Jazz Man peeks out from the folds of a favorite blanket. Two months after being rescued from New Orleans, he was feisty enough to cause a little havoc, sometimes literally bouncing off the walls of his cubby in exuberant dashes and occasionally leaving his precious blanket in the litter box.

● JAZZ

black cat named Teddy, and other feline friendships ensued.

The Jazz Man suffered a setback not long after, developing a case of ringworm that, because of his immune system problems, was hard to shake. He had to go into isolation until he recovered, but the vets and caregivers continued to lavish him with attention and affection, and a few months later he was back with his friends, ruling the roost again from the heights of the rafters.

A popular member of the Guardian Angel program that enables Best Friends supporters to sponsor needy animals, The Jazz Man soon attracted the attention of a woman named Gretchen, who applied to adopt him. He was all ready to go home with her, almost exactly a year from the time he had first come to Kittyville. But one last round of tests revealed a new and troubling problem: Jazz had a heart murmur, a condition that, given his other health problems, might significantly shorten his life. Gretchen was at first devastated. She had suffered some other personal losses during the previous year and wasn't sure she could handle the thought of another one.

But her second thoughts were only momentary. By the next day, she was ready to take Jazz to his new forever home. Gretchen renamed him Spumoni, reporting in his online journal that he was such a "sweet treat" that he just had to be named after the famous Italian dessert. Clearly a survivor, Jazz / Spumoni settled in quickly to his new surroundings, bonding with his new girlfriend, Munky, also a feline leukemia kitty. And despite some ups and downs, Gretchen was able to report more than a year later that one more Katrina survivor was still enjoying the good life.

CARING COMPANIONS

doctor in the cat house

The veterinarians and vet technicians at Best Friends pride themselves on being jacks-of-all-trades. On a routine basis they care for the two thousand or so animals at the sanctuary on any given day: dogs, cats, birds, sheep, goats, pigs, horses, rabbits, and even the occasional wild animal — from bobcat to eagle — who ends up at Best Friends for treatment and rehabilitation. Of course, some members of the team have affinities for certain species. Dr. Michael Dix particularly enjoys being called over to Kittyville for routine checkups or when a cat needs medical attention.

Dr. Mike was in private practice in Portland, Oregon, in 2004 when he and his wife, Elissa Jones, who had volunteered at Best Friends a couple of years earlier, came to the sanctuary on vacation to volunteer together. There happened to be an opening for a vet at the time, and it didn't take Mike and Elissa very long to decide to make the move. Elissa now heads the Guardian Angel program, and Dr. Mike is medical director at the clinic.

Most vets will tell you that the biggest challenge they face is diagnosis. Simply put, their patients can't say where it hurts. The Best Friends clinic is as well equipped as just about any veterinary hospital in the nation to run diagnostic tests, from blood work to X-rays and ultrasound. A seasoned eye also helps. With cats, though, it can be especially difficult to figure out what's wrong. Dr. Mike, who treats many dogs as well, sees distinct differences between the two species. "The hardest thing about cats is that they hide their problems more than dogs," he says. "Cats are quieter and more reserved. They tend to internalize their problems." And examinations themselves are more fraught with peril. "Cats are squiggly. They don't want to be examined, and they're harder to restrain. They're also quicker with their mouths and paws. And you can't trick them with treats." He's found that the best approach is to give his feline patients some quiet time to help them relax.

Despite the diagnostic challenges, Dr. Mike and the others have learned through experience what to expect. Feline leukemia, FIV, and other communicable diseases are fairly commonplace, especially among cats who have been living on their own as strays. The cats rescued from the hoarding situation in Pahrump, Nevada, also suffered from dental disease, ringworm, diabetes, and upper respiratory infections — all resulting from the poor diet, stress, and unsanitary conditions they had to endure.

The latest pharmaceuticals and alternative techniques such as acupuncture help many of these cats recover or live comfortably with chronic illnesses, but Dr. Mike never discounts the powerful medicine of compassion that everyone at Best Friends is fully authorized to dispense. "It's a different type of environment here," he notes, and the healing power of love plays a hand in almost every case.

Dr. Mike tries not to take his work home with him, but he does take his love of animals. He and Elissa have seven cats in their family — including his college cat, 16-year-old Stimpy — as well as five dogs. "They mostly all get along together," he notes with a laugh.

There isn't a day at the sanctuary when Dr. Mike doesn't feel privileged to be doing what he's doing. "The best thing about being at Best Friends is that you're part of something bigger to help individual animals, as well as animals all around the world. Even if it's been a frustrating day, there's always that feeling."

● SIMON

● COOKIE

The Caring Never Stops
lives of dignity and love

You won't find anyone at Kittyville who doesn't love cats right down to the very core of their being. But what does it mean, exactly, to love a cat? It means that, regardless of the physical or behavioral problems caregivers must deal with, day in and day out, they never waver in their unconditional caring. At Morgaine's Place, or the Colonel's Barracks, or Happy Landings, or anywhere in Kittyville—just as in all the other neighborhoods of the sanctuary—Best Friends' people surround their charges with limitless love, at the same time respecting, preserving, and uplifting their inherent dignity and encouraging their natural resilience. What's the reward? Time and again, the payoff is seeing abused, neglected, injured, or overlooked animals not only come back from the brink but also reclaim their true character. It's part of the Best Friends magic.

Lucy (opposite) is a notorious camera hog. Her caregivers think she's doing everything she can to be noticed — and get adopted. Pessa and Cashew (below, left to right) have been blind from birth but don't miss a thing. They now live with a woman named Mary, whose own failing vision gives her a special bond with them.

Spotlight on: **Mrs. Cotton**

Mrs. Cotton began her life misplaced by fate. This blue-eyed beauty with a snow-white coat was raised by a family who insisted on having her as an outdoor cat only. And since they never took her to the vet to be spayed, by the tender age of two she was already pregnant with her second litter of kittens. That's when she was hit by a car, which caused her to go into premature labor. She had five new kittens, an injured leg, and no nearby veterinary care. The family called Best Friends and drove her the fifty miles or so to the sanctuary's clinic. An X-ray showed that her leg was not only badly broken but also riddled with buckshot. Her family had no idea when she could have been shot, but they did say they had noticed her limping for some time.

Mrs. Cotton's problems didn't stop there. At less than five pounds she was seriously underweight, probably from having nursed two litters of kittens at such a young age. And her leg was in such terrible shape that the Kittyville vets determined it would have to be removed. She would be able to live just fine with only three legs, but not as an outdoor cat, which her family said was the only option for them. Faced with the realities they were themselves imposing on their cat, Mrs. Cotton's family asked if they could give her up into the care of Best Friends.

Care and love she got in abundance, not least because she was impressing so many of the staff with her bravery. Her leg was giving her a great deal of pain but she was not fit for surgery when she arrived. Soon after, her kittens were born, and she became a heroic mother, never hesitating to nurse her little ones, even though their nudging into her caused her to wince every time. And unlike many outdoor cats, who can tend to be shy, she had the sweetest temperament and a "purr like a diesel engine," according to Dr. Tara Timpson, the vet in charge of her care.

● MRS.COTTON

Devoted mother. Two of Mrs. Cotton's five kittens nuzzle in to feed. She never denied them despite the fact that their nursing hurt her leg, which was full of buckshot and had been broken when she was hit by a car.

When Q-Tip, Orange Julius, Quincy, Parfait, and Moonbeam were weaned (and shortly thereafter all adopted), surgery was scheduled, and Mrs. Cotton came through with flying colors. After a brief period of recuperation, she was moved into the lobby of the Kitty Motel, where she immediately and happily adapted to life as an indoor cat. She was so playful—snatching at her own tail, bouncing around, even hopping up onto a cat tree as if she'd never needed that missing limb—that it was hard for anyone to believe what she'd been through or that she'd been a mom twice over. Her caregivers started dropping the "Mrs." from her name, allowing this new Cotton to be more of the kitten she'd never had a chance to be before.

Just more than a week after she moved into the Kitty Motel, Cotton was adopted by a woman named Cynthia and her family, which already included other cats, a couple of dogs, and ferrets—as well as one very delighted young man, Cynthia's son, who took to cuddling up with Cotton every night. As for Cotton, she was clearly pleased with it all, and frequent reports came in from Cynthia about how well she was adapting.

The short time she was a Kittyville resident had made a big impression on everyone. Caregiver Cathie wrote to Cotton that Cynthia's report had given her "a little twinge of missing you. You were the best lady ever to bring such beautiful kittens to the sanctuary, so brave and sweet. I'll always love you and am so very glad you are happy in your new forever home."

Resident Status

That's the goal at Kittyville, of course: a forever home for every feline. It doesn't always work out that way, or at least not right away, but it's impossible to feel bad for those cats who end up spending their lives in the KitKat Club, or Jill's Diner, or any of the other well-appointed Kittyville residences. Take Bob, for example.

This playful black-and-white fellow lives in Benton's House. He'd been found in a box that was left outside a shelter in Page, Arizona, partially paralyzed and incontinent. It seemed likely that he'd been hit by a car, and although he regained feeling and movement in his back legs, he still had physical problems that the shelter couldn't address, so he came to Best Friends for special care. Part of his therapy involved going for walks around Kittyville on a leash, an activity he clearly enjoyed. As their first exposure to the world of personalities at Kittyville, new volunteers are often given an opportunity to take Bob for a walk. All one of his caregivers has to do is say the word, or reach for his harness and leash, and Bob comes scampering over. On occasion he takes more than three walks a day, enough to make even the most indulged dog jealous.

Out Bob goes with volunteer in tow, exploring the sandy terrain around Benton's House, nosing under mesquite shrubs, and scanning the ground ahead. A caregiver will usually have encouraged the volunteer to keep Bob moving if he looks like he's pausing, but more than one neophyte has fallen victim to this cat's clever stratagem. He will suddenly flop down on the sand as if every ounce of energy has drained out of him—but it soon becomes clear it hasn't. The next thing the unsuspecting volunteer knows, Bob has lunged forward and pounced on something with his two front paws. And there it is, wriggling in the dusty soil—a little desert lizard or gecko. A quick lizard rescue is now in order, and Bob is happy to have shown his talent as hunter extraordinaire.

Did someone say walkies? Bob, one of Kittyville's most famous residents, surveys the scene from his "tent" in Benton's House. But he'll be right at the front door waiting if anyone offers him the chance to go for a walk.

● CLAUDIA

Never too late. Native daughter Claudia was born at Best Friends and lived there for twelve years before being adopted. Shy around most people, she snagged her forever family by "talking" to them with a purposeful meow that seemed to say, "Take me home!"

Another longtime resident of Kittyville was a charcoal-gray girl with glowing yellow eyes named Claudia. She lived in the Jungle Room of the WildCats Village because she had a shy streak. She wasn't fearful of humans, just a bit timid and withdrawn, but over the years many caregivers and volunteers got to know her, inevitably drawn to her almost haunting stare. What many of these people didn't know was that Claudia had actually been born in Kittyville back in 1994, her pregnant mother having been brought to the sanctuary for care after being abandoned.

Claudia lived on, year after year, keeping mostly to herself. But then one day a couple who were looking for an older cat came by the Jungle Room, and Claudia started talking to them. There is no better way to put it. It wasn't just a gentle meow, and it was far from a complaining whine. It was more like she was trying to say something to Irene and Tonny, and she kept it up. They were smitten—and they got the message. Irene, who had been volunteering at other cat buildings, had seen plenty of other potential adoptees. But now there was no doubt in her or her husband's mind. Claudia, who was entering her thirteenth year as a Kittyville regular, was going home at last.

Sometimes things work out the other way around for a cat, as in the case of Six-Toes, who lived for years on the "outside" before coming to Kittyville for her retirement. The transition was a happy one for her—fit testimony to the welcoming atmosphere of the place. No one knows how old Six-Toes (who had an extra digit on each of her front paws) was when she first showed up near the pool of a resort hotel in Los Angeles, often frequented by movie stars. After a few days, she moved to a new spot near the front entrance, greeting guests with meowing and purrs, and sometimes lounging on an adjacent patio.

It soon became clear Six-Toes wasn't going anywhere, at least not voluntarily, and one of the staff agreed to take responsibility for her, feeding her a diet highlighted by leftover chicken strips from the hotel kitchen.

For fifteen years Six-Toes lived the celebrity good life. Then one guest complained about her presence, and the hotel management decided she would have to go. Her "mom" was distraught. She couldn't take in Six-Toes herself, but she knew about Best Friends and gave them a call.

It isn't always possible for the sanctuary to take in cats through individual requests, but it turned out there was a place for Six-Toes, and soon she was lounging anew, claiming the Kittyville laundry room as her own. No longer were famous faces all around, but the people in her new life made up for it with ample affection—and the occasional reminiscent treat of grilled chicken strips. Six-Toes couldn't have asked for a better ending to her long life.

Counting on rescue. The appropriately named Six-Toes lived for fifteen years as a stargazer, watching celebrities come and go from her hangout on the patio of a deluxe Los Angeles hotel. When one guest complained about her presence, a place was found for her in Kittyville.

● SIX-TOES

OPAL

Spotlight on: **Opal**

Cats come to Kittyville for many reasons, and their needs can be wide-ranging. Kittens in particular are often the victims of abandonment and abuse—a fact that animal lovers find completely baffling—and their youth can make their health especially delicate. Most disturbing are the times when a kitten is treated like so much trash, quite literally. One late spring day in 2007, not far from the sanctuary, a man was filling up a large roadside dumpster just before the trash truck came to empty it. As he tossed in more trash, he thought he heard a tiny sound coming from inside. He looked in and just caught sight of the tiniest little kitten you could imagine, struggling to keep her head up and mewing pitifully. Realizing this was a newly born kitten, he searched among the bags and other loose items to see if he could find any littermates, but Opal, as she came to be called, was alone. When he picked her out, he got some idea of why she might have been tossed out with the garbage: she couldn't walk at all, and she was covered in her own filth.

Opal's rescuer contacted animal control, and the officer who arrived took her to the Best Friends clinic, where veterinary technician Kerry Eddy got to work cleaning her up and readying her for a medical evaluation. She and the vets noticed that Opal had no tail, which suggested that she was a Manx cat and might be suffering from Manx syndrome. The gene that makes Manx cats tailless actually shortens the spine, which can cause neurological problems such as loss of bowel control and poorly functioning hind legs. Fortunately in Opal's case, though, the infirmities seemed to be only temporary. Although she needed frequent cleaning and had some trouble getting around at first, within a week she was much better and was soon using the litter box successfully. Her back legs were still giving her trouble, so she tended to hop around "like a bunny," said Kerry. But most of the time, the vet techs in the clinic

● OPAL

From trash to treasure. Little Opal was a newborn when she was rescued from a pile of garbage in a dumpster. Less than two months later she was adopted by a woman named Darcy, who had met her at Kittyville and fallen in love. A genetic defect makes it hard for Opal to walk properly, but she still manages to find a way to fly around the room in her forever home in New York City.

gave her a free ride anyway, carrying the tiny little thing around snugly lodged in the pocket of their scrub tops.

Soon Opal was ready to move in with the clinic's manager, Susan, and her husband, Jim, for foster care in a house full of other cats and three dogs. Two of the cats, Phantom and Casper, were neurologicals who couldn't walk at all, and Opal seemed to bond with them right away. She also liked to investigate just about everything in the house, flitting this way and that in her own distinctive, hoppity way. In her first online journal report about Opal, Susan wrote, "She is trying to be very helpful right now by running over the keyboard while I am typing, attacking my moving fingers."

Opal gained weight quickly and was able to have her spay surgery in due order. Although she enjoyed playing with Kerry's stethoscope during a routine follow-up exam, she was clearly eager to get back to her foster home—and little wonder. As Susan reported a week or so later, "Every morning Sadie, our old dog, waits by Opal's kennel so that I will open it, and then Sadie says good morning and promptly cleans Opal's face."

By the end of July, less than two months after her rescue from the dumpster, Opal was ready for the next big step in her life, a plane journey to her forever home in New York City. A TV producer who had been on assignment at Best Friends when Opal first arrived had fallen in love with the little package. "I can't possibly take a cat home," Darcy kept saying. But Opal proved to be just too irresistible.

She adapted to her new apartment home in Greenwich Village quickly, proving so energetic that Darcy claimed she could initially only get pictures of her when she was asleep; otherwise, she was just a blur. As for her "infirmity," Darcy wrote in Opal's online journal, "She's actually capable of jumping up, splaying out her arms and her legs in all directions, executing a full 360-degree twist, unassisted, midair, somehow managing to fly four feet across the room, without once touching the ground, and ending in a double-back semi-round-off back flip."

In her rare quiet times, Opal now sits at the apartment window watching the birds at the feeder. It's not hard to imagine, though, that she also occasionally catches sight of a passing garbage truck rumbling down the street. At such moments it's left for the humans to remember that one person's trash is often another person's treasure.

Spotlight on: **Rajah**

Cats with physical challenges abound in Kittyville, but the good news is that more and more willing hearts are coming forward to give them homes. Cats with behavioral problems, though, sometimes have a harder time finding their forever families. This may in part be because physical problems can be well-defined, and adoptive families can know in advance exactly what to expect; on the other hand, an aggressive cat or one with erratic behavior is by definition unpredictable, and the challenges are that much greater.

But there is almost always a way to make things work. The strategy that Kittyville employs includes not only applying large doses of patience and resourcefulness, but also nurturing and encouraging the accepting spirit that so many cat lovers seem to possess, even if they don't quite realize it at first. No story exemplifies the resulting rewards better than Rajah's.

Rajah is a Bengal cat, a high-strung breed resulting from crosses between domesticated cats and the wild Asian leopard cat; it usually takes about four generations for the descendants of such crosses to be considered true companion animals, and even then the Bengal isn't for everyone. Rajah started out feisty, but his original family exacerbated the situation by having him declawed. Many people don't realize what a negative behavioral impact declawing can have. It's actually a form of amputation and can be very painful, leaving the paws permanently sensitive. Many declawed cats, realizing they've lost their chief form of defense, react by becoming more aggressive, lashing out any way they can at any perceived threat. To make matters even worse, Rajah's family then brought two dogs into the house, and it sent Rajah practically over the edge. He would growl threateningly, hiss and spit, bat at the dogs, and even throw himself at them. And he took to spraying all over the house.

An ill-advised treatment with an antidepressant didn't solve any of the mounting problems and actually only warped his behavior more. His family had had enough and wanted to get rid of him. Most shelters aren't equipped to deal with such challenging situations. Had Rajah ended up at a local shelter, he undoubtedly would never have been adopted, and the clock would have run out on him. Fortunately, this is precisely the kind of special case Best Friends sees as its mandate. Arrangements were made to get Rajah to the sanctuary, and he soon moved into the WildCats Village.

The first thing the veterinarians at Best Friends did was to take Rajah off medication. They kept a watchful eye on his behavior and tried in general to keep things calm around him. It didn't take long for people to realize that he seemed to get along better with men and once or twice even hopped up onto caregiver Mike's lap. He also seemed to enjoy whenever a tour would come by, running up to the screening of his porch and virtually strutting for the camera-wielding visitors, many of whom had never seen a Bengal before. Rajah wasn't doing so well with the other cats, though, and would warn them off with his characteristic guttural growl. But he rarely

RAJAH

RAJAH

if ever displayed any overt violence toward the other residents of the WildCats Village; at worst, things tended to be left in a standoff.

Then, just a few months after Rajah's arrival, a man named Rusty entered his life. Rusty had never known much about cats until he took a tour of Best Friends shortly after accepting a position with the Bureau of Land Management as a planner at Grand Staircase-Escalante National Monument nearby. He was intrigued with what he saw in Kittyville and decided to become a volunteer. He seemed to have a natural instinct about its residents. "Each cat has a distinctive personality," he commented later. "In fact, I can't imagine adopting a kitten. It's the adult cats who have the personalities."

They say you never really pick a cat; the cat picks you. And that's what happened with Rajah and Rusty. Mike started to notice that whenever Rusty was working on Rajah's porch, the cat who usually loved to pose for the passing tourists paid them no mind—all his focus was riveted on Rusty. "He just latched onto me," Rusty said. In short order, the feeling became rather obviously mutual, and Rusty submitted an application to adopt Rajah and take him home.

The first reports back were encouraging. There were no signs of behavioral problems, and Rajah seemed to be happy with his new situation, being the only cat in the house. But then one day he caught sight of some of the members of a feral colony a neighbor was feeding in a barn behind Rusty's house. It seemed to trigger at least one old pattern: Rajah would get agitated and then start spraying in the house, which was filled with valuable antiques and other fine furniture. Things degenerated from there, even when the feral cats weren't in sight. Rusty was puzzled—and concerned.

Rusty knew that he could take Rajah back to Kittyville if the adoption didn't work out. It's a standard Best Friends policy—for the entire life of the pet. But he wasn't about to give up on Rajah. As he said later, commenting on his experience with the Bureau of Land Management, "One of the first things I learned was to respect the animals and their nature. I figured the same applied to Rajah. I just wanted to know why Rajah was doing what he was doing."

He consulted with the local vet but also called his friends in Kittyville. They suggested that he track Rajah's behavior carefully by keeping a journal and that he take a few other steps as well whenever the problem behavior exhibited itself. First, Rusty had the lower portion of his windows frosted so Rajah would never even catch a glimpse of the outside cats. When he did act up, Rusty would sequester him in the bathroom and leave him there until he calmed down, at which point he could come back out.

But the most important thing Rusty did was noting down every agitated moment and every incident of spraying, which were still continuing despite the steps he'd taken. After a few weeks, Rusty finally had a lightbulb moment: Rajah was going bonkers almost exclusively on Saturday evenings and Sundays, and Saturday was when Rusty volunteered at Kittyville. He was coming home smelling of all the cats Rajah had known—and loathed—at the WildCats Village!

Rusty loved volunteering, but he loved Rajah more, so his next move was never in doubt. Better yet, it worked. Rusty stopped volunteering, and lo and behold, Rajah stopped spraying and getting hyped up. It was as if he had said to his human companion, I want you all to myself and that's the way it's got to be.

It takes a special person, with a great heart and an even greater understanding of the inherent dignity in every life, to accept such a message and to take the steps Rusty took to adjust to the cat who had picked him out. And although Kittyville lost a prized volunteer, the larger mission had been served. Another cat was home.

The right man. Rusty spends a happy moment at home with Rajah. Rusty's patience and determination to do right by Rajah turned a difficult situation around. Once highly agitated, Rajah now seems at ease. "I know how to melt him," says Rusty.

CARING COMPANIONS

the "stinky tuna" lady

Dani Duncan has known a lot of the world. Born in Brazil of Lithuanian parents, she has lived with her husband, Douglas, in Argentina, Chile, Mexico, Canada, and several different parts of the United States. But in 1996, when Douglas's health required them to look for a place with a dry, pollution-free climate, they settled for good in Kanab, Utah. The clinching factor was that Best Friends was right around the corner. Dani had an abiding love for animals, and something told her that this would be her heart's true home.

A caring spirit had always led Dani to seek opportunities for volunteering, so she was quick to make her way to the sanctuary and ask where the need was greatest. Back in those days, cats with special problems were almost the untouchables of the shelter kingdom, and helpers in Kittyville's special needs buildings were few and far between. But that didn't give Dani pause, so the Kitty Motel — where geriatric, neurological, and incontinent cats, as well as those with feline leukemia and FIV, reside — became her stomping ground.

There are many more helpers now, but Dani still keeps busy with just about everything, doing laundry, washing food bowls, sweeping the porches, wiping down every surface, changing litter boxes, and handling special feedings for the cats with restricted diets. "I don't come in to look pretty — I come to work," says Dani. "By the time I leave, I'm bushed. But it relaxes me."

She still finds time to enjoy all the Kitty Motel cats and reels off a long list of her favorites: Devlin, Isabo, Crystal, Pokey, Foxie, Baby, and Wobbles, to name just a few. One little girl holds a lofty place for her. Genie came to Kittyville from the horrific hoarding situation in the Nevada desert, and was nothing but skin and bones when she first arrived. "We didn't think she was going to make it," Dani recalls. In addition to being severely malnourished, Genie had painful sores in her mouth and seemed perpetually terrified. But a combination of expert medical treatment and copious supplies of tender loving care brought her around. She still doesn't trust too many people, though — with the exception of Dani. "She and I have a good relationship," Dani notes with genuine affection. "I'm the only person who can pet her. And she really loves my stinky tuna." Every so often, Dani brings in a particularly odoriferous variety of canned cat food as a treat for the cats. "It's really, really stinky but they love it."

Many caregivers and volunteers in Kittyville will tell you that they feel mixed emotions when one of their charges is adopted. Not Dani. She loves her cats as much as anyone, but she's overjoyed when they get to leave the sanctuary and join a family. "Everybody is very devoted here," she says, "but to have personal attention on more of a one-to-one basis, to have a stable home — there's nothing like having your own personal human." She remembers in particular two geriatric cats, Regina and Taylor, who were practically at the end of their lives when they finally found their forever families. "I was very happy about that."

Dani believes wholeheartedly in Best Friends' mission to bring about a time when there will be no more homeless pets, when every companion animal will have a loving home. People like Dani are helping to make that dream come true.

ARABELLA

● BUCKLEY & BUZZY

Acknowledgments

The author wishes to thank all the people at Best Friends—caregivers, volunteers, vets, managers, and magazine staff—who contributed their expertise and their wonderful stories about the cats of Kittyville. This book would be only so many words without the marvelous images from Best Friends photographers Sarah Ause, Gary Kalpakoff, Clay Myers, Troy Snow, and Molly Wald. Special thanks to Kate Hartson for her guiding hand and constant support, to Michael Hentges for his excellent design, and to all the wonderful people at Sellers Publishing for making this book the best it could possibly be. And the biggest thanks of all to the cats of Kittyville, and to Twinkle, Aubrey, Carter, and Menley, who have, over the years, found their way into this dog lover's heart.

Best Friends
ANIMAL SOCIETY

You can contact Best Friends at:

Best Friends Animal Society
5001 Angel Canyon Road
Kanab, Utah 84741

www.bestfriends.org
info@bestfriends.org
(435) 644-2001

How you can help:

Become a part of Best Friends. You can sponsor one of the cats or other animals who live at the sanctuary, or donate to the general work of the society.

Volunteer at the sanctuary. Visit for a day or a week or longer. You can groom cats, walk dogs, feed horses, and much more.

Help in hundreds of other ways through the Best Friends network. See the Best Friends Web site for more information.

Adopt an animal from Best Friends or your local shelter. Make sure your own pets are spayed or neutered.

NO MORE HOMELESS PETS